Rosita's Robot

Katie Sharp
Illustrated by Danielle Jones

Rigby®

Rosita's mother gave her chores to do around the house. But whenever her mother handed her a list, Rosita would find something else to keep her busy. Rosita just wanted to have fun.

Each day Rosita's friends would come to the door and ask her to play outside. Rosita had not done her work, but she still asked, "Mom, can I go and play?"

Rosita's Chores
☐ Do Homework
☐ Feed Sparky
☐ Clean Room

Before Rosita could walk out through
the door, her mother told her,
  "You should get your work done,
  And THEN you can have some fun."

Rosita thought about how she could get her work done faster. She had an idea. A robot could help her! She gathered old computers, a telescope, and other gadgets.

Rosita's mother called out to her,
*"You should get your work done,
And THEN you can have some fun."*

At last Rosita built her robot, and it looked like this:

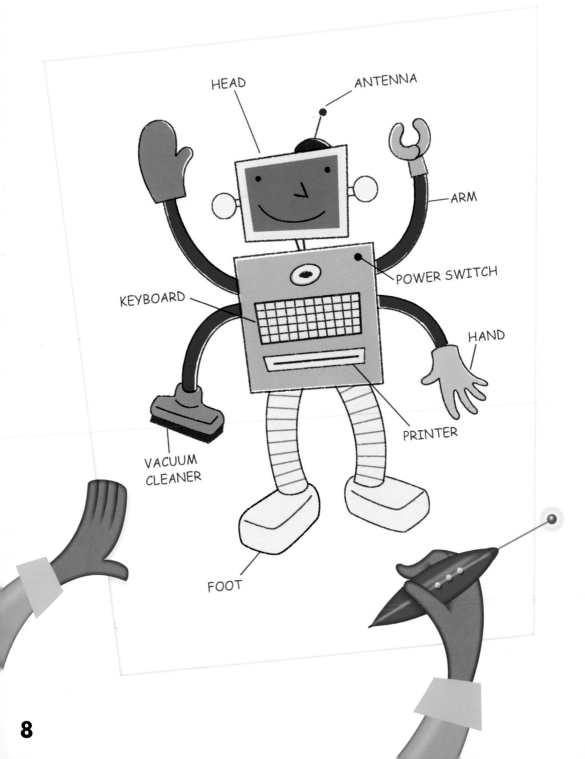

HEAD

ANTENNA

ARM

POWER SWITCH

KEYBOARD

HAND

PRINTER

VACUUM CLEANER

FOOT

To make her robot work, Rosita gave it a command.

"Let's play a game," she said.

Much to her surprise, the robot told her, *"You should get your work done, And THEN you can have some fun."*

"OK, robot," Rosita said, "I have to hit the books now. Let's do my moon report."

Rosita was able to look through the robot's telescope and see the big, round moon.

"I can see the man in the moon!" Rosita exclaimed.

"Light and shadows on mountains, valleys, rocks, and craters make the face you see," the robot told her.

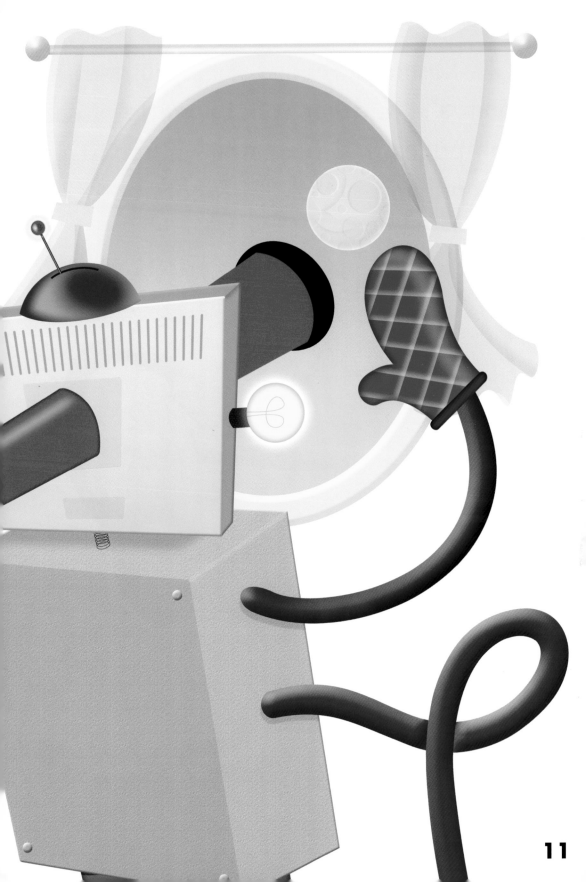

As Rosita learned more about the
moon, she told her robot what to write.
Soon pages and pages of her report
were printing out of the robot's body.

With her report finished, Rosita
wanted to take a trip. "Robot, let's go
to the moon," she said.
The robot told her,
*"You should get your work done,
And THEN you can have some fun."*

Rosita's Chores
☑ Do Homework
☐ Feed Sparky
☐ Clean Room

The Moon

Suddenly Rosita heard her dog
barking, and saw him running to her.
"It must be time to feed Sparky,"
she said.

"Robot, give Sparky his water and
food," Rosita commanded.

At once, two dog bowls slid out of
the robot's feet. One bowl was filled
with water. The other had food.

Sparky quickly ate his food and finished his water. Then he took a red ball in his mouth and brought it to Rosita.

"Robot, let's play with Sparky,"
Rosita said.
The robot just shook its head.
"You should get your work done,
And THEN you can have some fun."

Rosita looked at her list and said, "I have just one more thing to do."

She led her robot to her room and they looked around.

"My room is a mess," Rosita said. "Robot, clean my room!"

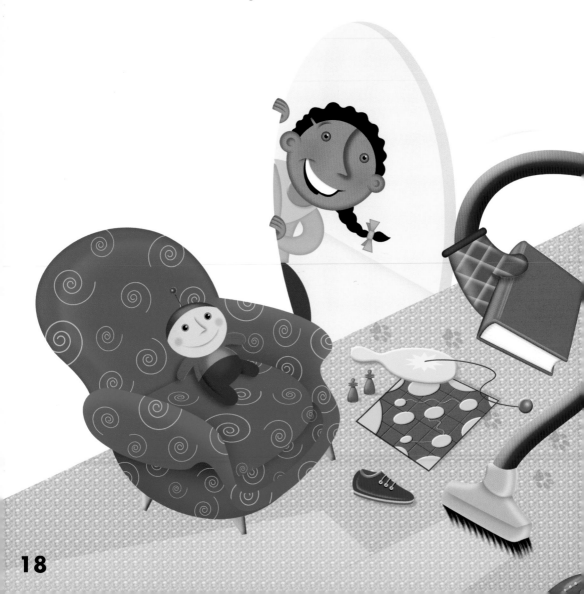

Within seconds, the robot was at work. All at once, it made Rosita's bed, put away the toys and books, and neatly folded all her clothes.

Then the robot vacuumed the rug and curtains. With another arm, it washed the windows. And with yet two other arms, it carefully cleaned the hamster's cage.

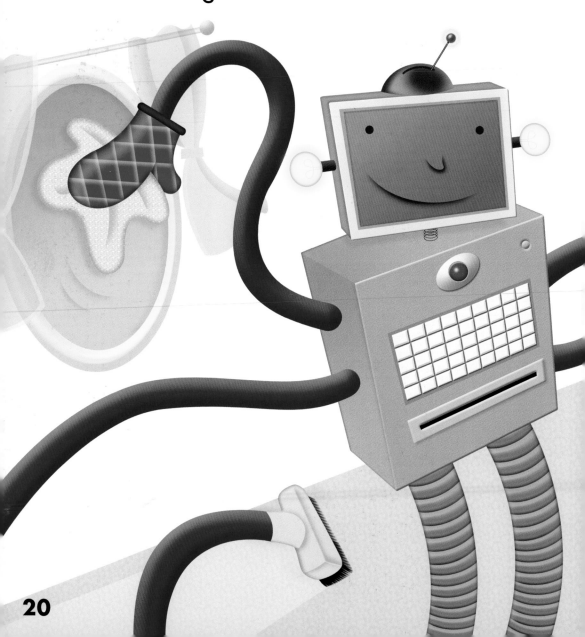

Rosita, dizzy from watching her
robot work, smiled and said,
"Now that my work is done,
I can go and have some fun!"

Rosita turned off her robot and ran to the door. She was finally going to have some fun! She grabbed her scooter and helmet.

"Bye, Mom," she called. "I'm going outside to play."

Rosita started to ride her scooter
when suddenly she stopped and said,
"*Now that my work is done,
I don't feel like going out for fun.*"

Rosita ran back, turned the robot on again, and whispered,
*"I don't want my work to be done,
Because spending time with you is so much fun!"*